KNOPF

75

YEARS·OF·PUBLISHING

Also by Amy Hempel

REASONS TO LIVE

AT THE GATES OF THE ANIMAL KINGDOM